THE RABBIT MA

THE RABBIT MAGICIAN PLATE

POEMS

by

JUDITH KAZANTZIS

SINCLAIR-STEVENSON

First published in Great Britain by
Sinclair-Stevenson
7/8 Kendrick Mews
London SW7 3HG England

Copyright © 1992 by Judith Kazantzis

All rights reserved. Without limiting the rights under copyright reserved, no part of this publication may be reproduced, stored in or introduced into a retrieval system or transmitted, in any form or by any means (electronic, mechanical, photocopying, recording or otherwise), without the prior written permission of both the copyright owner and the above publisher of this book.

The right of Judith Kazantzis to be identified as author of this work has been asserted by her in accordance with the Copyright, Designs and Patents Act 1988.

British Library Cataloguing in Publication Data
A CIP catalogue record for this book is available from the British Library.

ISBN: 1 85619 169 9 (hardback)
ISBN: 1 85619 195 8 (paperback)

Typeset by Rowland Phototypesetting Limited,
Bury St Edmunds, Suffolk

Printed and bound in Great Britain by
Biddles Limited, Guildford, Surrey

FOR
IRVING
WITH LOVE
AND GRATITUDE

CONTENTS

With love, January	1
Slovakia	2
Estate	4
The gardener getting on	6
The domestic woods	7
The passenger of the car	8
Eurydice	10
Jacob and the angel	13
Poor weather	14
The Earl of Modern Ireland	15
September, Kerry	21
Song of the Bull and Cow Rocks off Kerry	22
Feudal	23
Pandora Armistice	26
Death rhymes	27
Generations	30
Sylvia Plath's grave, Hepdenstall	31
Sisyphus who was Prometheus	32
The selfish one	34
Brooklyn walls	35
Autumn in Maine	37
New England fall, by motorway	38
Come to your dream home in the rolling forest	41
The Death of General Custer	42
Railroad station	44
Seeing everything	45
About lunchtime, Arizona	47
Towards nightfall, Arizona	48
The turquoise rabbit magician plate	49
East of the sunset, Arizona	50
Dusk and a Portuguese man o' war	52
Postcard from Florida	53
The Everglades	54
The Florida swamps	56
Night in Key West, a bit off the tourist route	60

Henny Penny on another day	62
Smart	63
The neighbors in Florida	64
Bounty	66
Mrs Bai	67
Night in the parking lot of El Rancho Motel	68
What the doctor orders	69
The avocado tree	70
The avocado tree in winter	71
Sapodilla rental	72
The wind	73
The American woman at the ruins of Tikal	74
The tourists	77
Swimming up the Amazon	78
Leaving the table	80
Nicaragua and the old man in the white house	81
The discoverer	82
Temple of the Codz Pop at Kabah in the Yucatan	83

SOME OF THESE poems have been published in the following magazines and anthologies: Ambit, Stand, Verse, Bete Noire, The Honest Ulsterman, Prospice, Oasis Press, The Rialto, Slow Dancer, Writing Women ('The passenger of the car' was originally published as 'The fogbound forest'), Key West Reader, Key West Review, Angels of Fire: an anthology of radical poetry in the Eighties, Leamington Poetry Society Pamphlets, Other Poetry, Affirming Flame anthology, Tribune, Cardi News (The Committee Against Repression and for Democratic Rights in Iraq).

With love, January

They are stretching out like shadows,
some of these nights. The love whose skirts
you in your last letter kissed,
I lift them for you.
Thumbelina squatting on her lily pad
writes to the swallow, because in his
smoothie lapels, nacreous tiepin, shot blue tails
soon he'll fly that 'sweet little thing'
far from – Ah, your fingers stretch longingly
over me, I'd have the odd wrong note,
it would be luxury to say
'go slow, flier,' you winged piano man.
Or have you thinned to a mobile of swallows
by midnight, over the truckle bed, through
my aching: wood flecks?
Not so simple. I smiled, when
your letter called me all sorts of names.

Slovakia

We will love in the uncertain lift
at the Dukla, we will mesh,
we will quiver and wobble,
two lions and a cage going down.

Please, more decorous
on the high street. The cathedral
demands it, a soprano descends
the loudspeakers over the gardens
innocent and rich as snow.
It's the organist, who sings
behind her gilded machine.
Girls and women haunt
their golden Our Lady.

Coal dust burst into our room
at five o'clock this dark morning.
The cathedral walls are apricot,
its elaborate spire blackened.
A freight train passes –
thinking of your grandparents
though this train carries the brown
coal to Prague and Bohemia –

we think, entering the painted
synagogue, with its congregation
of only eleven old souls to dust
the Torah and lovingly intone
to us – yes how tall iron
stalls conveyed impurity
all the early hours north
to Poland. Your young aunts, owners
of childish faces. Thirty trucks

pushing over the road endlessly,
black gold going west
after all, in a cold evening,
teenagers waiting, whistling
by the barrier in cheap denim.

Estate

On the estate the figure
of Pangloss rides on the hill
on a tiny white mule, and downstairs
in enraged trees the half-wit owner
drinks to his own death,
forever handsomely
breathing his last. No, no!
Pheasant chicks, half-grown,
bred for the festival of feathers
falling on Pangloss like
iridescent manna, they run
like Road Runner between my feet,
they twitter into the kitchen,
to the sun falling on my jug
of wild flowers, no more idea
than me lost in a space module,
their pinwheel eyes static,
stopped clocks; unfocussing
further, they run off
under white saxifrage, into black-
antlered, glossy headed knapweed
and with dignity parade,
are lost in walks of scabious
(sunken shipwrecked violet
like the sea mistily riding
the other side of the doctor riding
the spine of the downs, so small) –
Sad chicks, truncated, half bald,
don't they have a thousand senses,
a thousand and one stories
they'd be happy to tell?
Like a dinner companion
the red sun napkins itself in mist

and along his ridge my merrily
fat brother wobbles.
I wave, and evening steals along behind
and swallows the day and the year.

The gardener getting on

I know three evil names,
ground elder, bramble, and bindweed.
One apes roses for thorns, one strangles
while playing Angel on its trumpets,
one is less drama but comes up
stolid like tank regiments
reported out of steel roots.

My old chums (a worse pack of weeds)
crow how heavenly, a lush green riot!
Do they, I wonder, do it spitefully?
Seeing my fingers knotted and flushed?
Or to comfort? I'm not so sure.
She's near to her final ground,
our elder – is what cheers *them* up:
my rusty gold chrysanths cut-throated
and lost. Comforters, your ground
elder lives. That's the red finger
that claws down as undegradable
as plastic, I promise, to get a hold

and wrench out the evil ones.
I'm tougher: my blessed flowers
queue in the earth for their true
time of colour from the sun,
and feed from the rain gravely.
I love to work and mind this garden.
There'll be no riots, lush hellish
or green heaven. I'm more
leathery than God or Satan.

The domestic woods
– *for my mother in illness*

The independent cat
walks through the domestic woods by herself –
The grasshopper jumps –
Who needs a hand?
Neat and sleek as a brown
gnat catcher dancing along the fence:
the picture sang.

In the mirror
suddenly the bird fell dying from the air,
the cat now lost to freedom
in rain soused fields
where tempest
felled oaks and barred paths.

A tremor
seizes the mirror of her picture –
they were saying, they were stammering –
Flying along to her
through the clouded air, bird empty cloud –
Through the wingless woods of the
bird empty air –
they were stammering, they were stammering –

Curse the oak-tree, never swear
by the oak-tree, the unfaithful,
the cat hangs in its hempen hair,
fluttering,
spilled across paths.

The passenger of the car

We flew,
myself bolt upright,
comfortable,
like an ivory duchess
on the luxurious dark blue back seats.
(The chauffered duchess
he accused
and wanted me to act up to).
I tapped his shoulder.
The dark blue chauffeur
frowning like a triton unfountained.

He drove,
hair slicked back with salt sea,
a large low forehead
furrowed like a wake,
the sweat like pearls bouncing
from his frown into his streaming eyes.

He flew
like a purring ship
through a fogbound forest.
Scrub oak: you should see
the bold dark green leaves
like children's cut-outs,
off such wisp-like trees.

The night flew
the pearl car
past a border of pearl saturated
salt-preserved mansions,
each for a duchess,
each gunned into the little oak forest,
each its own pearl.

Such flawless trim.
The cut-out leaf becomes
indefinite:
no dark nor bold leaf,
what is there
but a comb of mist sorting the hanks
of a bald and lame wood?

Because of the frailty of the trees
– I had mislaid
through tinted glass
a more precise sense of their growth –

trembling,
after much consideration

because I was frail,
because the seats were as plush as dew

at length I opened the weighty
dark blue door to the oak forest.

I flew
like a car of fog
up from the sea
and pouring inland in thick waves.

Repeatedly, repeatedly,
I tapped his dark blue shoulder.

At length, after much consideration
because I was frail,
pearl-like,
I opened the weighty door
into the low wisp-like scrub oak-trees.

Eurydice

Eurydice never died.
It was Orpheus who went down
eagerly to the city of Hades.
He walked like a bandsman
with a broad back and the slung lyre
that had charmed all living things.

Birds, animals and Eurydice
followed the singer, whimpering and pleading.
– She held up her arms,
glowing in sun
but his back was turned on her,
he lost himself in the cloak flaps
of sumptuous Persephone
who patrols the buried walls.
The mouth of the beast Cerberus
fed him down.

A venom bit Orpheus, maybe
some snaky envy of his own tongue?
At any rate he died, and
the birds, beasts and weeping woman
climbed in a sad file
back through stalactites and rock lumps
to the small high-up sun.

Eurydice hoped to die,
to join him; but instead,
seeing her white face,
which was grief, not death,
I was sorry for her
and I whispered, go to the shore.

I followed her discreetly
as her tears sprang down
on the brown and scarlet leaves.
We trudged through
a great plane-tree forest
to the sea. She took
the seashell, broken and chipped
but still iridescent
and zigzagged with amber words
as I'd set it for her;
it lay by the wave.

And that way,
pressing my shell to her ear,
bending to hear against the breaking
roar, as I'd suggested,
she heard her singer.
The dolphin and the seagull
flew from element to element
while Eurydice heard
his voice, Orpheus murmuring
marvellously from under the shore.

Under the slamming of the waves,
the young man murmuring to her:
I am here, here, my love,
in a glittering town.
I stand up in a tower,
I see all Hades –
With my lyre
I call out the illustrious beauties
of this place, the beat
and hustle of its fires, the jewel
in the small flame, sea-blue
or sea-green, Eurydice my love.

She cries
into the zigzagged shell:
Orpheus come back – you're
wrong, you're in hell,
Orpheus my love, come back.
But the shell gives out one song
whispering, ecstatic.
Each minute a wave
roars, to block it.
Eurydice walks home
through scarlet leaves
and the cracked stumps of trees.

The shell
sits by the tidemark.
I followed her ten times to
that amber whorl and ten times
her expressive eyes
said, as she bent: my love,
my agony.
I was myself hopeless and wiser.
I hurled the shell
out to sea on the autumn tide,
for the fish to crowd in
and catch the blind corpse's voice
sing of fire,
and gawp and gape
in their pure shoals,
nosing for the singer.

Jacob and the angel

He flew at me like a ghost in a top-hat
but I went at him like a champ.
I doubled my fists, in my sweatband
and my singlet and long black tights
and my elastic sided pumps.

We didn't wrestle,
he carried me,
he carried me along on thin air.
He spread out his grey white wings
like a swan or a goose or an aeroplane
aloof on miles of solid air
and I his underbelly, his breast, his fuselage
held like the under half of a clam-shell.

Pluming me in my body
as heavily as a feather or
the believing finger of a tornado,
the angel carried me along under him
by this finger, I holding to it,
upholding him like an intelligence of air.
We didn't wrestle,
the wrestling was over,
this comrade beat and thundered and whispered
inside me with his breadth and length
whispering, my Jacob, my main man, my woman.

Poor weather

At dawn, rounding the head,
the water a flat calm, and then storm
brushing in, veiling in.

Spray pushes and pushes on the breakwater,
utterances opening and continually
fasting on stone and ending,

rambling onto stone and ground,
sipping in estuaries
through tunnels slanting back deeply.

Yellow flag for cowards like me,
he turns back, tethers his delicate dinghy,
the wind expending on the bay,

and gracefully drinks of his daring
in the florescent pub that evening.
The boat urges itself on its mooring.

The Earl of Modern Ireland

1

All billowed to noble queenly or
   kingly size,
beeches, copper or green, sycamores,
limes, oaks too, though elms
   have gone since.

Cromwell's man's desmesne;
   the grass: stinking green lush.

Jackdaws: clack and flutter-tumble –
   Spider servanted, jackdaw butlered
– It's a mercy the whole place doesn't burn
down in a chimney fire one night
while His Nibs is in Dublin, London.
   Others have.

Whee – here comes the mist
   up from the lake, breath and arms
     urging out of the wetlands.

2

Blue-eyed Euro-farmer Michael

                  'one moisty
morning at dark-eyebrowed five, in the darkness,
I drive up to collect my cows for market, load
them, go on to the next place where I have

stock, and impatient to see not a light,
the farmer snoring, cows moving dark in the
farmyard. Ah hell. A figure in the dark darkness
looming, it's Father in his dark black cassock
all in the dark and wringing his hands eleven
times, we're in terrible terrible trouble but
somehow unable to spell out the trouble.
Weeping the farmer who keeps my herd runs
shouting and his wife weeping and the little
children weeping and he jabs me in the chest
with his shotgun in lessening dark and jabs
and jabbers, I can't take it any more, I'll do
away with myself, prodding me with the barrel
and Father in darkness dancing by willing but
helpless – Off my heart I pull the barrel of
the shotgun, the farmer yields it up sobbing
and I uncock it, unload it and now to me the
greying light announces my beautiful champions,
my mothers all in calf, £70,000 worth so I'm
telling you after dinner in the firelight in the
library, and the farmer, God's Act of a
betting man, has for the bookies sold 34 cows
in calf while I was away in Australia'

                        as he stands the backs of his
thighs before the red logs among the fragrant
leather of His Lordship's great 18th Century
library, 34 cows you'd not miss at a glance in
a herd of 400, in a herd of 73 in rising sunbeams
out of the dark of the night there would be bound
to show a little lack.

3

His Lordship to give a lecture
at Ballynamuck, on the French landing.
He has no notion where or when
or who to ring or who rang him
                              in the first place.

At lunchtime on the day invited
Ballynamuck rings, they're having
a Mass for the dead and stone blessed
and no lecture. Himself gives hearty thanks
                              and stops swotting.

4

On the grassy lake at the walk's end
lives the lady of the lake
and her white spouse the bull swan
and one grey maiden, whimpering.

To the food island orange with lilies
came to her five brothers and sisters one night
a mink: that swam beneath them one by one
and bit off and made off with each sleeping head
and left the five corpses floating
and now she whispers up and down all day.

5

Fiddle de dee of the young trees . . .
The Earl is obsessed with slurry.
Sued for polluting the river
he instructs Messrs. Murphy not to appeal
against that scocious trout-fishing magistrate:
'. . . in my fifty years on the bench'

Mr Murphy puts in the appeal.
His Lordship's fine is doubled.
De profundis of the full-uddered oak-tree . . .
Cows full-uddered, moving and swaying
muck-arsed, paper labelled and rubber docketed,
one being on each side of her black face
branded 20 in satin white hair . . .

6

His Lordship's Folly

He brings her to bed	He brings the youthful stream to her new bed, to her bolsters of day-lilies and hart's tongue.
He rejoices her	He rejoices his bride with bluebells and to the embrasures of great roots he devotes the primrose.
He adorns the way with bugloss and other flowers	Make diamond the bride's path through bugloss, through ragged robin. Let her run through conifers.

She caresses him   He builds her a foolish island
                    full of amethysts and orchids.
                    She holds it in her arms.

He dresses her   Boned by an inlay of mosses,
in gold   corsetted by the gold quatrefoil,
                    the stream glides to her dress.

And she takes him   Like a wizard he has struck her
to her   with his wand and he has called
                    and she flows on all his sides.

7

The tourists come, stepping gingerly.
They have paid their pound –
for slurry and the primrose?

Through a leafless rhododendron
they press on and here are swans!
Vikings on the water

mink slain, dignified, eaters of algae,
children of the Vikings on the lake-water
beating tempestuously –

8

Skeletal forms do not pester His Honour,
never hit him in the boyish face
like bats loosed out of their cave
by someone's indecent mistake.

So he is lucky – the State of the Nation
is fairly fat and European
and for each Anglo master of plenty
no longer a hundred go dying.

Such luck! And why so forgiven?
They pay their pound in money
of the mint salmon of conservative
Irish wisdom: which gives him the place.

9

*In the event of victory, hold on to your
rifles, as those with whom we are fighting
may stop before our goal is reached. We
are out for economic as well as political liberty.
Hold on to your rifles.*

    *James Connolly to his Citizen Army
    before The Rising, 1916*

September, Kerry

At three waking and looking
                    through floral curtains
the hurricane gale's bled out
the sea's barracking and quaking
                    the stones merely
and a stiff penny face the moon stares hi
travelling at the full and at a standstill
her Indian yellow coiffure, her
                    gasoline aureole
turning round on the cloud crust
                    never burning –
Stare to the pack below, wolves in the bay
                    restless and snappy
or white hares
       their long ears flared and sprayed back
as they breast in, smartened by the moon.
But later I want to lie down, to sleep,
       burrow into the undercut of dark mountains.

Song of the Bull and Cow Rocks off Kerry

The sea horn swings, swings the sea tail
                sea udder sways

Out beyond seagulls
                hump, skip Bull and Cow
Other side of the mist yard, far small
        in Atlantic water meadows
      bellow the black Bull and the black Cow

Sea udder sways, sea horn swings
                swings the sea tail

Feudal
(from Bresson's *Lancelot du Lac*)

A child is tying brushwood –
        whisking like a blackbird
  head
      feathered on its lightning stem
    eyes glimmering in starved skin
whiten
        like a horse hauled up to halt
                in the wind

Out of the wood   out of the wood
       he states: I've lost my way –

    Leaves break at the shoulder
              of the charger
   at a leg's cylinder dangling
    crooked in chain mail
This is Escalot – the crone replies

After the wound   her mother's curing
   their hovel   he dying   she
  hunched   the girl eternally
  scuttling   for ever bringing in
                  kindling!

he heads off on the enormous
     castle flanked   star headed bay
        she scuttles this time
          to seal the last hoofmark
with kissing

She like a squire had stored
                    the armour
His blood clotting like a villein's
   His eye far from
              eagle   wolf   man
   slitting and slamming the glades from
                    the palanquin
     of the stratospherical horse

     Eye   far   not starry white
                               ablaze

   Mind curing in the candle

God's tongue – the lance   God's cloud –
                  the shield, casque!
     The ton weights for me carried
   by the sweet lord, O merciful Lord!
in whose protection from those giants
          straddling   axing the woods

as they themselves fall to oneanother's fury
  – whatever their rammed weight catches

He in whose protection   I am
   a white pebble   a soul saved

He picked me up, then out of the thicket
                        came
   a wild boar   with an iron snout
                – a white stare
Lord Jesu they lifted up on the gallows tree

Kissing the plate-like prints
        of a giant horse
            Before its sallies and courses
                      stones fly

  each clover obeys
not with its root, but with its green stem

Pandora Armistice

Pandora rich as Midas but nowhere so mean
sits by the step each day and sells her flowers.
For free this street-seller allows you to dip in,
pushing the basket forward when you gulp, Ready!

You know how the regiments can fly up in sheathes,
but death can fan from a head of deranged pistils.
You must edge round these clusters, and the blooded mash
of poppies, and fainting lilies, and stalks fixed like bayonets.

You must poke your fingers past the flowers of the grave
and hook free the layers of dolls lying underneath,
yellow and brown dolls and black and ivory
done up in rows of gauzy gold and silver.

Free them and they'll fly up like fishes
and make their commune between her breasts like peonies
and like bees ride into her armpits
like foxgloves, and like butterflies into the tulip

of the earth blooming, the bulb giving forth
her calyx of husk, light, honey, salt.
Through her treasuries white poppies slide and slip.
We all died. It was all nonsense. We should have lived.

Death rhymes

1

Nightshade, nettle and dock
Death stands inside the clock
I take one pace
I brush his face
Nightshade, nettle and dock

2

You are in russet
And I prefer velvet
We share our luncheon tray
Death smells the roast
And edges up close
And snatches it clean away

3

Death and I went up the hill
When I began to loiter
Then Death jumps round
And throws me down
And puts me in his halter

4

Death and his mourner and me
Rowed out one night to sea
Our trip had been longer
If I had been stronger

5

Death be merciful
Death be quick
When you jump out
With flare and stick

6

Death jump down
From off the wall
In my bowl
Come break your fall

From all the high hill
and all the clear skies
You'll seep in
And white my eyes

7

Death and his mourner
Sat in the corner
Joking and playing at puns
Such as 'fair me' and 'fear me'
And 'no me' and 'know me'
Crick-cracking the joints of their thumbs

8

Mister Priest called a feast
Mrs Earth spread the cloth
Mr Death had the best
Mr Mouse filled his mouth
Eating cold cadavers

9

Old woman, old woman, old woman,
    quoth I
Why toss so and labour
    and sigh?
I'm cleaning my coffin of spiders
    and flies

Note: from Hickory Dickory Dock, Miss Muffet, Jack and Jill, Three Wise Men Of Gotham, Jack Be Nimble, Humpty Dumpty, Little Jack Horner, Mr East Made A Feast, There Was An Old Woman Tossed Up In A Basket

Generations

A distressed mother rejects another
distressed mother rejects
another distressed mother rejects
another distressed
another

another   another

tries to heal the sore place
deep   under layers of
hard sharp wound tissue

hard

Sylvia Plath's grave, Hepdenstall

          A thick
waved slab, mottled grey,
regulation end-paper.
A yard of grass
tight-lips this dead will.

What orientalism, what wealth
has been drummed up
on this skinned ridge.
Mud, harrowed back, fresh.

On stage are more
garrulous tombs, black
and shining with fear of death.
Minutely dated, nothing spared.

'Even amidst fierce flames . . .
the lotus may be planted . . .'

I lose the words, among
spidery rain falling on thin top-soil.

Even amidst such flames
herself she dusted down to this
cleaned out grate.

She governs me
with her still furious flowering –

Therefore, her steely horses
proceed, ice white
white heat –

Sisyphus who was Prometheus

Sisyphus thinks it's a crappy job, oversleeps.
Night and dreams divert him and take his attention.
Illuminated by a wet dawn
the boulder moves lightly up the mountain.
Moss grows, soft as a cat stepping.

*

Bald, a tonsil in throat dark.
Once again Sisyphus sleeps in
the monster's dusk, run off his feet.
All day all day go on go on yes yes nearly
But not – Omigod you motherfucking

*

Temple of Demeter configured
of marbles, limestones, clays, gemstones, granites.
Where the cycad roundly untongues above
the mirrorless beetle, lizard's dropping eye
and ratchet lichen. Greatly it rains:
green grows the conservatory; with inside
fogs netting and beading the red herring-boned
tiles, pipes, spiral stairs, cliff-faces,
tree-crowded hilltops, panes
drop herding to drop under the stratosphere.

No column, no pediment. It worked out
like a cat quartering a hillside speechlessly,
moving up or down with intent.

*

What's happened to fire? From the above dank
and homely symbiosis, he comments, the sun
has been totally excluded. Sisyphus swears,
in God's vent he found something unparalleled,
that wasn't before and can't be again.
Making a straight line for it.
Thing unrepeatable, far more than earth grain
or liquid drop: a flicker he saw come
once and to infinity, one and one and one
along oil or coal or wood edge.
He saw its edges and where the next
ringlet or wave came into its own life.
Therefore make a central place for his straight
capture; nothing clanks round for ever
without a motor. How forlorn
to fear and to give the fire-carrier
this boulder-peddling to mock his fierce grasp.

*

How can he allow a single water-drop
to run down, a mere stone to find its own level,
he who has climbed his brains for fire
as I have, has timed it, his heart beating
for the whoosh, each occasion with such work
to the crater's edge, detonation after detonation.

How can I allow a bare stone day after day
to lose its balance and to finish up
in the same trough? Nothing can climb
this hill without me. Day after day
I am crushed with the duties and the sadness of God.

The selfish one

Is this selfish, the stoat
that charmed my ribs, the way my knees
unpin for the mother of pearl wrench . . .
Kneeling . . . Yes, she sees it so.

– To be that marble pippin
twirled, teazed by tongue and teeth!
Integument crisp, acid sweetly
she'd lay hands on, and not

peck to a scab, whistling,
or, as a tree past bearing,
slap the apples, thump,
even the ones unripe, to the four winds!

This a minute ago; around
itself the minute makes a film
as a raindrop proofs itself to rain.
Then one flood, three decades crystal.

Inside the flood an apple
sank down, saturated, and the
pip fruited into the flood bed,
fully possessed with the liquid

of bearing. And therefore the fruit
better rinded, not against lions
and tigers, not against the stoat
of love: against thievery of flesh,

against pecking, against calluses of
careless let-fall. Rise, O lady
of longing. What long flowing
to bear and grow a selfish tree.

Brooklyn walls

– Many Egyptian, Hellenic, Aztec,
Renaissance, and made of paper.
The gritted tar-paper adorns the little shack.
Stone fortifications rear on the might
of Blois, its rubbled and dimpled blocks.
Their hills rise to battle slits or slog up
to a cottage gable and dormer
perched fifty, a hundred feet, overhead,
or plod merely to hulk. Pale blood-coloured temples
step up slashed with bone chips, nerves
and the white titbits of marbles and limestones.
Pediments gable and gargoyle,
gothic, regothic, barothic and rococo,
imprint with prolonged texts, man high
the easy to read names in passing of Plato to Jay Gould.
Upheld by pillars like bridge stanchions; or
they guard the single mansion, dumpy
as bottle palms. Pillars to sit on earthquakes:
lonesome, or Delphic groves of threes, fours,
yard Doric, Ionian by the metre, Corinthian
bits stuck out and grape swags in heaps.
To walk a block, ceramic porch floor tiles in
grass green, sky azure, crazy Mediterranean pathways.
Each side, fountains of polymer, water frozen
in the hose tap. Upstairs the stars cut diamond
cold by night and Santa yells in fibreglass
as big as real, popping his bulbs across
the mackerel shingles of the adorned shack.
Bigger than real, in fact, and bopping along
brighter and faster than anyone else's
speed of light dare rock around the block.

The big heart of Brooklyn is red, red.
Expansive red or roan, pepper and salted,
liver and salmon and raspberry and mulberry;
also banana, lesser caramel, treacles, cringing
beiges and demolished greens, the curtain
of Giant who lives here? Black poodles
live in the castle. Hoarse and vivacious, voices
in lobbies complain of snow and fixed wealth.
The horizon stands stoic.

These are the red cliffs of the Navy Yard blocks.
Here the poor live hole by hole, like puffins
or sand swallows or troglodytes or the poor;
hole by hole though the burrows are square,
twenty stories up, a table, TV and chairs.
Unpedimented, ungargoyled, these red cliffs
of Fort Greene were built for southern Blacks
to come make World War submarines.
A large chunk of Brooklyn's red heart
since those days, unchanged; not a corner
even for a swatch of paper sidings
(grey and creamy chiselled to stone of Blois)
to take off the edge and impart style;
here are people with strong backs to walls
roach and rat riddled, here are people
who joke and shout and skate to the stores
on sidewalks of smashed bottles, garbage of stars,
diamonds for the ladies; here
are the carriage and kitchen quarters
of the castle of Giant Who and the poodles.

Autumn in Maine

Mermaid, instep of blood,
swanning in the wood;
maple, alizarin-haired,
bouffant, my bareback rider

counting her flowers and cloak
of rubied sequins away.
Spore, turquoise;
rosettes of the obsessional

lichen creep to clothe
the whistle white birch muscle;
fungi, ringed and beringed
like the trees. Of whose finials

chrome yellow or Indian yellow,
in my hand matching up leaves.
Berries multiply, fruiting
the scarlet abacus of the year.

New England fall, by motorway

1

Swinish cars include us
blundering and panning across holyland.
Translucent on rocks the stained glass oaks,
the maples, bless the drivers impartially
who do or don't give a monkey's
for what our six mean streaks replaced
nor for these great survivors of the carnage
now bitted and bitten back each side
by – yes! us! the creative lords!

Between their blue leads, the weighty
laterals of spruce, cedar and pine,
these stained glass scenes in the lives
flick by us – the jewel box clerestory
mixed up with grand episodes of the nave.
We're in such glut, storming Maine to Boston.
We see no soul but blurred types –
that bend rose or golden heads.

When I was a child these crowds
sang in spheres, sometimes.
Such crowds, halleluia makers upside
down in real gold leaf on an apse
or spread etiolated and gigantic
over a transept arch, both pillars,
and coming on high to a Christ or
dove or to a flying prayer of ten fingers
lined up like palings, or better,
like ten silvery pale saplings of birch:
birch alive in a forest,
lifting themselves year by year,

generation by generation,
in praise of what I praise too . . .
as we zap on through: their land.

2

Inside the acute white noon
maples and oaks oscillate, the dulcet
and bristling jump of light: orange, orange,
crimson. My eye is the harpooner; but better,
the whale harbouring into its eye-mouth
the lights of the floating world.
Sap fails: to this looking-glass eye
middle radiances flow from the tree instead,
the inner molecules break outwards
along the branch, twig and stem line;
they surge the dykes of leaf veins and ribs;
all brim, then light gliding
away over the levees, the heart
pours in reds and yellows through the limbs,
the lapping outwards of waves through
five-pointed or seven or three-pointed hands,
the tree burning,
as timed for light as oil and a wick.

3

Turning the street corner the sugar
in the maples, the sap syrup,
melts on the glance in lemon sherbets,
in wine gum leaves, in wine
splattering and pooling into banana gold
five-lipped offering saucers.

As one cloud will shine like a snowdrop,
maples conquer the street for light;
clouds of golden or pink powder waved
out of a puff, out of a bedroom window
and hanging along the air at moments.

At intervals maple leaves dress
bodies with steady volcanic interiors.
They shed such starlight, endurance,
lordliness, a gas jet . . .

Lightshades, layered horn jerkins,
chain mail in rose doré, orange
bird god cloaks, the glass mantles
we had once for gas . . .

In Boston
       in Marlborough Street
                      in October
when evening comes by my window

why light the lamps?

Come to your dream home in the rolling forest
– realtor's ad, Cape Cod

O rapture running free, letting your hair fall free
in the little falls of the yellow-leaved oak-trees
of Mashpee on Cape Cod on the South Cape –

O peach and nasturtium jacuzzi
off a vast bathroom, off a master bedroom off
                                                a vaster lounge
with a settee colossaller than the Rockies but softer –

above it on the wall a screen print of a lean
                                        and mutilated maple leaf
blue and nasturtium, next to that a sailboat
like a mutilated maple leaf sailing a sea of matrix dots.

These presentations and representations –
they peer through acorn proof glass
into the little falls of the finial pointed oak leaves –

(this year the leaves fall twice and once finally –
The bronze galleys plunge, the sunbeams cease to row
like oars flickering off fleets of bronze and gold.

A pond: a leaf in continual pirouette
like an elderly promenader at the branch end;
or entranced; as if the air was a glass case
and transfixed gold or ruby were the tracery
of a shrine that stands inside and that used to be revered.)

O now I, in my sailboat, sit on my mountains
under my own maple leaf inside my glass case
and my rapture and I peer out and the rolling forest is
                                      my very wonderful dream home.

The Death of General Custer:
programme on American Public Television

*The man. The myth. The sombre
mystery. Of the last stand.
Will we ever know? Probably
not. Exactly. Till the end of time.
Linkman explores the headstones
of the warriors of West Point:
his tanned face and grey thatch
intelligently and somberly pause in the afternoon.
So many buried . . . Yet
General Custer's fame everyone knows.*

His tombstone's as high as a Cheyenne's eye.

Infant or old, bones into wide grit,
the panned grit of the fast rivers –
the bones go like a flood into the soil,
one with the dog bone, one with handfuls of chicken bone
one with turkey bone, deer bone, Indian bone
distributed like fertilizer.

Earthly flesh, infants sky-high like round birds off
the arms of breastless women
opening their mouths to

out of the arms of headless women

out of the screams of the bugle,
its shrill melancholy still plays for us
safety and rescue in our hearts and minds.
Like fluff blown up before the horse hooves
the bloody parts of newborn babies rise, rise up,

kneel down before the troopers, rise up before their bullets
and kneel down before the scream of the advance.
Weeds are chopped back,
the Nations are herded to the fast river by

that tricky mystery, that dandy, that
perpetual enigma of our history, brilliant strategist:
who got himself killed and America's first defeat.
By hard assembly of bullets used,
ballistic experts have worked to show the
exact spot of the tragic fall.
Now I, linkman
and my friend the acute East Coast scholar
advance to the Bighorn question:
– General? Was it here? Or there?
Or down in the valley or halfway up
or for sure standing yellow-haired flourishing
his sword on the hill?
But exactly. We'll
probably never know till the end of time. How.

Linkman, your tones
behind my ear dot perfume
of the nation's old blood stench;
because the people dare not build a tomb
as high as a white man's eye
to the hundred thousand infants
whom Custer hated, whose
bird bones cry
inside the trumpets of the nation.

Railroad station

All life is little railroad stations,
he murmured as he bent over her
like the older Gary Cooper, to say
goodbye; though he wore no hat,
no soft hat. Then he hitched up his
dun-coloured Brooks Brothers suit
over his furry stomach – how
she would miss nosing her way up
or down his furry stomach. Sure,
she answered under the low cirrus
dun-coloured in the orange lights
of the platform, all's arrival and de-
parture; looking just as wan as a
girl in a film still set in Minnesota.
Still, she blew a kiss or more
as the train ranted out, on its way
to connections she with her single
'55 Studebaker did not aspire to
(he was the worldly guy); and felt
her thin hair drawn back
in the starlight into a pony-tail.

Departures are worse, she thought
suddenly, acidly, in the station –
master's torch's gleam and regretted
he'd gone, she'd like to have called
that last thing, just on the hoot
of the train and seen, as he'd bent
to light up his pipe in the carriage,
his eyelids flicker in the glow.

Seeing everything

– in the Sculpture Garden and the National Gallery of Art, Washington

A butterfly going down Washington
passed me and the Calais burghers,
ignored Song and chose to rest
on the Indian woman who dozes like a mesa,
whose lap is like a hanging valley,
a massive worker taking her own time finally.

The butterfly – its own image drifted down:
a sky plane trail lost low –
in an unknown tongue made a golden remark
against the black velvets of Miro commas,
some offer of irresponsible do-nothing
I refused as soon as saw.

I see everything in the city: finally
the conquering light behind Rembrandt's mill.
But lastly, his baggy eyes say lustrously
to me – me! Why this world?
Why continue in these flat lands?
Why suffer so at the foot of the sky?

I tried to brush by; no luck, and worse,
he was three hundred years dead, with
that look, and I have the tenure
and none of the skywise gift
of the golden and black insect, and
I was talking of my despair and listening,

blind and dried, to these glossy pigments:
dreams of the large eyes and kind face
of Mynheer Rembrandt once, who told me
after a while to go back and try again,
like a butterfly, like a woman worker.

About lunchtime, Arizona

Between somnolence and the sun
a hornet (a crow!) plonks, thrums,
blacks out the languid mountains.
I cringe, let fly a handful of fingers.

Trembling back, a thumb of emerald
evening feathered, the hummingbird
seeks and sips at, wagging,
a red-hot poker flower lip; it coasts
unflowering oleanders to the desert,
hooping the draughts like a bee.

Towards nightfall, Arizona

Birds take turn on the pate
of the saguaro, swapping riffs and ruderies.

Within its body, entering and hopping,
flicker, screech-owl, finches

two or one, are pillowed on water,
nested from the crystal cold,

cooled from the sun's rocket.
In six o'clock shadow hoboes

with stove hats, pipes ahoy,
hitch-hiking arms and a bad case

of jokes – You can't get there from here –
trot on the rose-red canyons:

I'm no beggar and no god (a spiny snug,
green-skinned, boot-capped, soft-

centred, abnormally tall, blurry
on the height and visible for lives.)

Rotted, lamed on the sill of cities,
a dumb-sign: Slow down.

I keep your desert.

Note: the flicker is an American woodpecker

The turquoise rabbit magician plate

At that eatery that was starred highly
and the mesquite outside burnt
with columned and pre-praised perfume
but nevertheless the smell handled me,
though now metallic and lateral jaunts
through climates later I forget:
O magician I cautiously bought whole
– Oh with what care I brought it back
and the glancing smell of your feathered spine
and trumpet, the amateur hooked back curtains,
the glaze – My own eyes I can feel
as whole, owlish, hazel, as randomly spotted –
How did men invent you – O sir, a woman!
Nothing is whole. At this last moment

distinct and concerted,
your lumpish sky, starred, your black
childish musical instrument playing rapidly,
an Apache woman painted this in tradition.

East of the sunset, Arizona

The west's in a powerful termination,
a fiery cheek, a raggy and ferocious old wino
fast highballing down. But in the east
the sky conceives dawn,
the sun burns to pallor,
is delivered of rose coral,
rose bloom behind the rock jut
(here where we stand: famous for red-gold
in which our faces, our hands are masked);
bloom opaque as pond ice
from twilit north to north reflective south –

(south, north divide what's
founded on blues, dispassionate,
from its ranting opposite;
one spread-fingered pole
shadows the other
through halfway emerald, topaz, lapis)

– Exulting without tone or contour,
a mile upward without shadow, breathing
out of the violet twilight's broadening garden.
Till porcelain, without shard or announcement
or fire, melts; or a sail is plucked
and tears upward. Hard to time
the confinement into blue, into the blue-
black apex, a rock chimney capped
for the time being before stars . . .

Bore down through black hoods
of firs, rerun troughs heat tipsy
and cracking to zero; down to the desert's
workings, inducted through gulches
by old saguaros. By leathery violet gauntlet
one hands us to the other.
We fly on the road, we run our fingers
down a spine of moonlight.

Dusk and a Portuguese man o' war

We are in the tropics. I'm sorry to say
    what slews round the corner
is no fun: winningly, slidingly
    under its indigo puff sleeve
under its beacon blue eye, its arms
    outspread to me.

The lengthening sea is a sapphire sore.
    Radiant glitter: a bloom
on the face of Gabriel. But this is
    barely healed surface tissue,
reams of plastic recoiled and recoiled
    round diabolisms.

Stir it up with the spoon of the breeze.
    I remember Coleridge's sailor's
jig; the fires pivoting round the hull
    some day or night or not-light,
a stationary process. This is
    to be afraid of the least touch.

Postcard from Florida

A seamless hacienda, sun and moon
forever in the heavens,
stars large, fronds lapping my feet
(the only fly: my flea-bitten feet).
This wicker artwork is
tidal waved by dew, never
by rain. Snow never ever!
The swimming-pool chuckles madly,
an uncle in the yard, with bliss, bliss here.

Merrily do our dogs gnaw and bark
on our laps. I am selling flamingoes
on sofas and you are selling shells
soughing heavy metal, pouting
of lips or hibiscus. All the flowers blare.
I am hopping along.
Everyone here drives large clean jeeps, forever.

The Everglades

Where the strangler fig
    clasps the tourist
        by his red neck   finally
where the pointed snail
      glows   a skein
          a slipping lick of cat's milk
          down a trunk
          a pure white jumbly
and a dozen jumped
      out of our cars to gaze

South the 'river of grass'
    flowing to the brown Gulf –
        Such a sun-drained yellow
lions and lionesses might fly out
      from bronze lairs after gazelles –
But look down   and small fish
    steer round the grass blades
They feed
        in the transparent underlay
zigzagging underfoot to the rills

Water hurries the stem, wind
        strips the grass head:
a sky of all directions swirls
        on vacant and stupendous levels –
        Drive drive on
Leave the white snail
    wending the red trunk
      of the braided gumbo-limbo tree

South   the grass makes
                    headway to the Gulf –
Look down   small craft
                        steer by gold marker posts
                                coasting
limestone: piebald   naked and
                                    clear
down to the old crushed volcanoes

Expunged from some sweating hammock
of hot   hard
            iron hard mahogany trees –
Unstrangle a breath   redneck
                                and gaze

how minnows
                sail through
                            the gold grasses

The Florida swamps

1

In the up-current the heron places its breast
        as plump as the wind
                abreast of a white schooner

    – the hollow-boned and feathery model
a surgeon makes of balsa spars,
            an eye surgeon whose hands

invade and exquisitely alter
        minute territories and seas

– as the red prop-roots of the mangroves
      lance and clean scour the sea
   and loop stitch its many islets around here,

over and over stitches
           along the water hem
  or along the cuff and hem of an island –

which is cut so badly, ruined by rib roots,
       as you stare in, looking for a centre,
any idea of a self to this swamp:

      the self is historic only, to be seen
looking down a black pupil
           which expands and you see

to the back country past the lens, and there
   a comatose flicker, the past continuous
     chilling your brain, played over

       and over again, the old movie, old movie
to sickening exhaustion, no start,
            no finish, a white full-winged

heron lights on a mangrove, a candelabra
       taller, only a bird's leg taller

than a billion others (the ants,
          the bees of the swamps).
   There too a loggerhead turtle

swims along in the current, lifting out,
       lifting its jaw periodically, like
an old boy mumbling sunshine.

2

          Feeding on wealthy and lavish rot
inside cocoa brown and bottle green shallow

the mangrove forks the sea,
  smoothes, slowly bursts, hatches into
            its third element, the sunny air,

then through the air it curtseys out hoops
       back to the stare of the sea; engineers
          a crinoline to lift up its

scrawny grey waist clear of the salt.
   The new island is sewn into the sea.
      Seas fill, maps after all exquisitely alter.

3

The Seminoles hunkered down here, forced off
        earth by repeating armies,
                hanging on in stilted shelters.

Only to them, or beggared whites – or to
        herons, ibises, spoonbills – you suppose
                the tall upbranching tree becomes a flame

of its kind, and present continuous
        rubs and salts down in their palms
                into usable strips,

jars, pots, hollowed out skiffs and thatch
        for the roof, to which known currents
                bring them swirling home

                or else they are swirled out past the
mythic and historic island of
        the gathering of the wind-breasted spirits –

way out to the islandless ocean which is
        an end and placeless.

4

But your attempt to find land
        where there is no land but
                merely islands bottomless with sea

or your attempt to find sea
        where there is no sea, no horizon
            but merely lakes inland

where there is no land
        but roots kneeling on roots bedded
                on the corpses of the lavish water

in which fish can be nursed and oyster –
        shells are wheedling scalpels to
        flesh and foot and leg, and snakes linger –

the drain, the sink-hole
        in short, of the United States, into which
            the losers were stuffed –

it still is a blind green iris to you –
        Yet how the whole
                operation replays later

with gestureless and changeless
        blindfold and lilting vision and consolation
            long after your own eye

has caught in far off dazzle the first/last
        marker post, the out finally,
            as if that uniform grey chainsawed

        wood oblong were the first outpost
on the suffering edge of the eye, of reason and sense.

Night in Key West, a bit
off the tourist route

The earthquake bass
of someone's sound system passing.
The professional age old thrum of cars
passing along Trueman Avenue . . .
to sleep and to each other's arms.
In sunshine the sidewalk
reeks of gasoline, that high scent
your lungs take a pinch closer
to home each day.
Round chins or gaunt bone
turn to you out of the jammed visitors'
luxury homes from homes –
Which nest's the truer? Asking yourself
to while away the last fragrant block.
The 'American love affair with the
automobile, in the shape of
the gas guzzler' steams into
the end of US 1 all winter.

At two a.m. insomnia
in Margaret Street; the well pump next door
is clocking on, clocking off
and we are land girt
but a sea-going siren harps
on the wires beyond the sapodilla.
A neighbourly row just shrieked: Fuck
OFF! Fuck OFF! and dogs
are milling with tin gusto,
the moon on black and white
and fleas and tics, and far and near
WEDDINGS CATERED FOR   FREE SNOW REMOVAL

the garbage truck sucks in
rubbish like hot soup
and constantly scalding,
digests hysterically gate to gate.

Behind these country noises
you have the smooth running of Trueman Avenue,
the internal combustion engine,
say, the odd U.P.S. truck
rocking up Route 1 to Miami all night.

Henny Penny on another day

And again the sky above us,
Henny Penny was heard to say another day.
Contemptuously the animals
told her to shut her beak,
stop her nagging. Rocky Cocky tiptoed
high and touch-tested the sky – it's OK,
he growled – folding his wings after
a short affirmative grunt: It's hard,
and well above us, it'll never fall,
a good stiff wodge of carbons, CFCs,
nitrates like that. Pass the bottle.
He drank, beer streaming down his wattles;
the sea mouthing into the farmyard puddles
through the five-barred farm gate
into the troughs, stalls, pens, pond
in the corner; but Cocky Rocky stood
on the dung-heap in the steaming rise
of gases, crowing Gung Ho To You,
as fit as a king, as a fiddle.

Note: in the folk tale (which ends in the jaws of a fox) Henny Penny claims the sky is falling and Cocky Locky and others give advice

Smart

I opened our smart casement.
Down half a mile in the forlorn lands
there a two year old girl stands,
covered with mud, wavy brown-haired, chubby,
red on her forehead, on her mouth,
                                        chin, neck
as if she's been dipping into jam
and her hand will be smacked for it.

On those roads
dust crouches in the marshlands,
                                        in the mountains.
There appear whole new dunes in the desert.

In the cloud's abdomen
I open wide one more time,
not now for the drift down of bombs.
Clumsier today, it's packed lunches
labelled hastily with my sincerest wishes
I lob to the reddened child:
chewing-gum, beef in barbecue sauce,
                                        other comforts.

Note: in March 1991 after the Gulf war the US Air Force airlifted spare food from US Quartermaster Corps to Kurd refugees fleeing the Iraqi Army, after an abortive uprising encouraged by President Bush. Not long previously the Allies had been 'indicting installations' throughout Iraq, including in Iraqi Kurdistan.

The neighbors in Florida

Hey presto, Jackie popping
a brawny white-haired head
gloomily over the fence:
Hi! Come swim with me!

I've envied from my side
a pool, a fjord, an ocean . . .
It turns out four strokes up
and two of them down, and sink.

Immaculate haired she chats
and coasts in her rubber ring:
'D'you remember New Jersey?
The exact shape of this pool!'

Her waving palms are sawn.
They browned and sank and died
of the Lethal Yellowing.
Down here we're living scared.

Jackie explains, the sun
is cancerous and huge
so we shut our door in May
and open it up in Fall.

We breathe with A/C on
indoors all summer through
and we bring up our wheelless bike
to work out by the bed.

We drive to get the stores
twice weekly at Wynn Dixie
and we chill the Buick hard
just like a Jersey spring.

And then at Sunday noon
to Pronto on the Rocks,
they do a terrific brunch
if you don't mind Donald Ducks.

She floats me down a gin:
You guys will love it here
just the way we do!
She bops inside her ring.

Bounty

Drawing curtains of a simple French restaurant
the cashier spins dimes to the poorhouse opposite.

At such ratios one may lounge in attractive disarray,
ringed hands. One admires the effect wryly, then fast

aerobically, turns from the mirror smilingly;
having been brought up in schools not to be vain.

To accept, yes. With God lost in space one must seek
to love self. Half the heart knows itself, devourer,

the other ventricle pumps little amounts through
the system, to keep the toes and fingers twitching,

for working when required. The brain, that is to say
the proprietor, needs to take on help in the high season.

Mrs Bai
– for Carolyn Forché

A young woman squats in her doorway
in the sand-floored alley
outside the iron-ringed factory.
Her six month old sleeps in folds
of her sari of apricots and gold.
Her husband died of lung related
diseases last year, and before him
his father, and their daughter of six.
She waits for compensation.
She is ringed by debt.
The factory is surrounded by junk.
What manager will not throw away
a cog-wheel blunted, dull and bent.
'I get dizzy if
I try to pick up more
than three buckets of water.'

Night in the parking lot of El Rancho Motel

Two muscular toms, twin ginger.
One squats upright outside the wheelcap.
One, leg outstretched, eye swung,
inquires the bumper, star spangled.

Laid on a feather of the dark palm,
a moon trembles, a minute crescent,
the salver of a weighing scale.
Crickets beat tin spoons.

Unreachable under the chassis
of the silver car, holed up for how long
a smoky and creamy she-cat
lies at ease and licks her forearm.

What the doctor orders

But doctor, there are innate properties
I think. How in the tropics in April
the heat's growing, not any psychic fever
but inside the balloon hot air is pumped in
daily, and more of it tomorrow, replacing
the trick or treat breeze. I want
that wind like a lollipop. I look for it
down the street as I blunder, remembering
the angles that bounce the draughts off the sea.
I rely on skin licks of yesterday and not
only on twinned eye and skin which squint
and prick for shade. But that most of all
I am wading in the dense, denser balloon
which is pressing in, not stretching, so that
I myself am the thrumming skin.
At this point I'm frightening myself again,
you say. Merely, as I look ahead,
my heart in double beats, I want the man
who is ahead of me, and taking no blind notice
of the sun. I think it is so huge
it is a flap, invisible. It is slicking him down
in front of me, he is becoming a shimmer.
And you will say, I have pulled this skin
over my head, contracted, forcibly wrinkling,
and what I must do is open and let the heat swim in!
What I must do! I want to be cool.
There are climates in this world
with their own extremes. Perhaps this shimmer
will turn around and come to me and ask.

The avocado tree

You are sweeping the avocado leaves
                        off the decking.
I am thinking in bed, just on my waking
                        but this can't be fleshed out.

Not so quick, not so easily, but one season
                        when your little house
has baptised itself for its hundredth year.

In the ferocity of April sunshine:
leaves all night-time scuttling
                        down the tin roof
and these gutter canoes (in a day's downpour)

give branch to the tuberous flower –
                        abyss yellow sea-stalk –
as you might find waving far below you.

The avocado tree in winter

The avocado tree like a spider
        branches out of the gravel,
a fair spider, dangling with beards of moss
      grown in air and from bark tags

and lengthening their frizz whether it rains
or whether drought attacks the most bulbous weeds.

An umpteen-branched candlestick to our path
        through here, through the house
          through the garden
     through, sweetheart, our birthday garden
full of casual violet indigenous weed-flowers
and stinging caterpillars who do not sting to death
     but roll riverlike by, all fur.

Sapodilla rental

You could swear it was the parrot,
two-tone viridian shivered with rage
catapulting out ass over gizzard
and calling up such cataclysms as to disturb
everyone, chased the hawk
out of the sapodilla tree,
though in that furnished and svelte tree
for all the birds that dance the quickstep
there are mirrored rooms inside
after a few gins at dusk and before
the sun has stared itself down finally
to a last and profound reflection
that behind the tree against the sober East
desires you swig again
to the intercourse of light and dark –

No, it was the parrot
sordid and shrieking like a haunting
or the luminous nose, far down
over White and Fausto's, and scudding
to the scam and misery of a roost
among the breezeblocks of the airport gulags.
While the ermine robed and bar-breasted hawk
with imperturbable anxious eyes
and something staid round the beak like a trap
begins on the dappled under deck of the sapodilla
upright to watch a cat newly appeared
and stalking the weeds of the long waste lot
under the composed, rosette-figured apartments
of the sapodilla tree.

The wind
– for I.W.

        Well, a tree
noisy in the breeze, wood yawing
but not under painful pressure, just
the opposite. And, a wind. Masses of leaves
swelling but not rushed off
in the other direction but into the wind,
into the cave of the four hundred mahout winds
trumpeting and trumpeting. And then,
to insist the blossomed tree into the source,
the caveman's fire, the warm belly
of the elephant mountain. But this is not
to fall or burn but to offer, love and have
my pleasure in the porterage of the wind.

The American woman at the ruins of Tikal

The afterword of dawn rain
is talking its way down through the leaves

at the beginning of the poem.

One hummingbird, present and not present,
in a wide glade entranced with crickets,
crickets like a city telephone exchange,
like a hand pressed down on a car horn,
like pigs grunting.

With orchid eyelids
serpents walk on thrones. They nurse
giants with eyes like grindstones,
with teeth like tank treads –

In the heat of the afternoon
they lay papaya and heads
on altars higher than the highest mahogany.
'The beautiful jungle is so friendly,'
chants the American woman on her way
up to the moon,
to the next part of the poem.

On her way up to the moon
a fly made of green marble, a frog with pink hands,
tell her, you are safer than a street here –
She springs up in old sneakers,
bean necklaces and her skirt
strange with buttercups and daisies –

On the third step of the poem
if she climbs without chanting,
she'll meet the cat o' the forest,
a fox in orange light
mothering its three stumble-pawed cubs
with a frown of yellow eyes
and forepaws like a vase, long stemmed –
Ix Ch'up, Young Moon Woman –

Dead eye, spit in your eye,
the altars shoot for the same old identical
blood-red sun, a sitting head across
the vast and transient repossession of the leaves,
ruffling and squawking.

– If the voices surround her, the spider monkeys
considering their slow high wires
a hundred feet into the ceiba tree,
and the toucan making a small streak
in the white cloud like an ibis, but
the yellow half of her is all mouth –

The moon beginning to ride
the shoulders of the poem like a silver backpack
is a weight she wants to carry off
in her arms, if she carries on praying hard
out of her unguarded forehead
and curls sweat-blackened –

Climbing down,
feeling the ringing darkened road
to the campsite: halfway,
the black and red-haired coati mundi
stands its ground, replacing
its paw on a leaf silently;
and stringing its back like a bow
it lopes to her

like a comma in a long ending sentence
as it curls to the heart
of a dark but light remembrance

(as she spreads her skirts out
in a glade that smells of deer and jaguar)
and it lays its dark light triangular head,
its light head, its yellow
and triangular eyes
in her lap of bromeliads and orchids,
on the last lap of the beautiful
and the friendly poem of buttercups and daisies.

The tourists

Who are the tourists?
One sits, writing his postcard at a window
in Quito, before the big procession.
The city is wet and white and grey,
full of Indians from the mountain
to watch the stories of the Great White God.
The Spanish priest complained, once,
the Indians have no word for guilt,
they had to be taught   guilt
This is Jesus de Mucho Poder
                      Good Friday's Man.

Swimming up the Amazon

'One hundred yards,' white thatch
chuckles, slumping down by his thin Joan.
'Well done, Denton,' she gravels.
'Be there by twilight,' he chuck chucks,
his curly chest of a chestnut colour loosely
heart thumping. 'Scotch?' 'Naw, humidity
level, I better not, doc said –' 'S'right,
Hon.' 'Jeez . . . Boy! Boy!' The nicest
old boy on Earth. Decking its flow
above Manaos, beating up against the current
into far origins. One day they jaunt
in rubber dinghies into tributaries
to barter and swap smiles with tribes,
worrying after at dinner whether they'd
ecologically interfered. Old child
of timeless, head in a cuchacha
so familiar it's rockaby, still
in his birth caul, keeps crawling
in a blue pool, in mid steamer, in mid-river,
crystal as blue as Windolene, his eyes'
own blue, machine bearing its cog
in Windolene upstream to the river's
brown birth, fountain by the Andes wall.
River with watered palms lined waving,
steamer with watered potted palms waving.
. . . To vanish, a flight of parrots
crying on the rails, frightening his heart
for a leg of luxury; and they fly
and vanish into the decked leaves as if
they never had cried, neither had
cried hullo nor goodbye, and the trees too,
felled as if they never had waved
at the folks and the swimming-pool and the boat,

as if in magic time this cruise had wound
through fading wonders to catch
the last sights. Denton is nearly there;
by twilight, he growls, chuckling
over Scotch as brown as the bringer itself.
Behind him and Joanie, closing in
on the bend, bulldozers haul away the forest.

Leaving the table
– *for Harold Pinter*

You told me
what he had told you in the evening
at supper in Managua
– what they did to one man –
I forgot his name, his importance
– he was someone fairly important –
His body was found on a hillside,
hacked up, with the genitals
stuffed in its mouth,
that they did this to women,
to their breasts following rape.
That he'd lost priests, catechists, health
workers, professionals of various kinds,
as well of course as the thousands
of peasants, campesinos, campesinas.
That my kindly
America has funded such
art out of the City of Despair?
Out of Gehenna? Can I believe
in any of this – something
I dreamed up that you breathed
to me malignly over the table.
Yes but we had left the table,
and illegally wandering,
we came to a hillside where
the great folk of the city
ordered the bleeding
and the dismembering of their servants
the many poor –
those who'd said: No more.

Nicaragua and the old man in the white house

Over the mountains, over the sea
there freedom lit the morning star
and grew the flower upon the tree.

Oh well armed thieves in the night came leaping,
they slit the throats of children sleeping.
Oh who has armed the thieves so well?

A buzzard, a jackal came over the hill,
one circles, one sneaks, each to a child,
the beak and the tooth are handsome steel.

Over the mountains, over the sea,
oh who has armed the thieves so well?
Feather of steel and hair of steel.

The bird and the beast came over the hill,
they came to the house all shining white,
we've done your bidding, we've done your will.

Old man, old man, the children are dying
over the mountains, over the sea.
Smile, old man, for many are crying.

In dark he smiled, in night he smiled
and dark fell on the morning star
and wrapped the land in mourning bands.

Smile, old death, or shout or rage
but still by mountain, still by star
the growing child shall come of age,

the growing child shall come of age
over the mountains, over the sea.

The discoverer
– for 1992

Cristobal
is standing
on a hill of many colours,
royal blue and canary yellow,
jungle green and Christmas scarlet.
All around him stretches a world,
sea, hills, shores, vales
of such bright tints and intermingled hues,
and deep in the vales, out of clefts
fog filled, milky, tensile,
arise aromas, beguiling, murmuring
of palaces, cities, banquets, the chambers
of exquisite intercourses, feastings,
consumption of joy effortless, in sum
the whole perfume of happiness.

Cristobal
the new discoverer
prods the rotting crust of the dump
and finds a glass bottle no one else found
and sticks it in his plastic sack
                              for resale.

Temple of the Codz Pop
at Kabah in the Yucatan

A huge iguana is the pediment
(suddenly look up and there it is, lounging).
One mask above three hundred rain god masks
ogling with their Puuc double vowels
and their boxed eyeballs the flat winged
skeletal-stemmed acacia forests.

Red earth, laden with lacy fern leaf
where the Mayan children and thin
chocolate brown pigs and big red-wattled
turkeys walk.

Inland sea-skin, sea ripples baked
as the desert: the biggest dragon outside
a Chinese screen of one stroke,
meaning a nostril in the smoke
of water falling.

As tender – as baked meat in a stew.
It elevates its nose to the horizons
much as Chac's three hundred nose-
trunks unscroll and protrude: stony
Long Nose swatting up the Sun: three
hundred hard memos to the water demon.

Note: Puuc is the Mayan language of the area
  Chac is the Mayan rain god